Editor: Penny Clarke
Consultant: Richard A. Hall

JACQUELINE MORLEY
is a graduate of Somerville College, Oxford. She has taught
English and History, and now works as a freelance writer. She
has written historical fiction and non-fiction for children and is
particularly interested in the history of everyday life. She is the
author of *How **would** you survive as a Viking?*

RICHARD A. HALL
is Deputy Director of York Archaeological Trust and has
directed Viking age digs in York. He is the author of *Viking Age
Archaeology in Britain and Ireland* and *The Viking Dig*. He is
a Fellow of the Society of Antiquaries of London, and a past
chairman of the Institute of Field Archaeologists.

MARK BERGIN
was born in Hastings in 1961. He studied at Eastbourne College
of Art and now specializes in historical reconstructions. He also
illustrated *Roman Town* and *Inca Town*, earlier titles in this
series. He lives in Bexhill-on-Sea with his wife and children.

DAVID SALARIYA
studied illustration and printmaking in Dundee, Scotland. He
has created a range of books for publishers in the UK and
overseas, including the award-winning *Very Peculiar History*
series. In 1989 he established The Salariya Book Company. He
lives in Brighton with his wife, the illustrator Shirley Willis, and
their son Jonathan.

Created, designed and produced by
The SALARIYA BOOK CO. LTD
25 Marlborough Place
Brighton BN1 1UB

Published in 1999 by
Franklin Watts
96 Leonard Street
London EC2A 4RH

Franklin Watts Australia
14 Mars Road
Lane Cove
NSW 2066

ISBN 0-7496-3298-4
Dewey Decimal Classification Number 948

METROPOLIS

VIKING TOWN

Written by Jacqueline Morley

Illustrated by Mark Bergin

Created and designed
by David Salariya

W
FRANKLIN WATTS
NEW YORK · LONDON · SYDNEY

CONTENTS

INTRODUCTION

Why not visit a Viking town? If that strikes you as a good idea then obviously you need a guidebook – and here it is. Like all guidebooks this one starts with a little background information.

The Vikings lived in northern Europe in roughly the equivalent of present-day Denmark, Norway and Sweden. What we call the Viking age began in the late 8th century when these seafaring people suddenly began making coastal raids on more southerly peoples. Raiding was followed by settling; before long there were Vikings living in France, England, Scotland, Ireland, Iceland, Greenland and Russia. Some even reached North America although they did not manage to stay there long.

The Vikings earned a terrible reputation abroad for savagery, but in fact only a small proportion of Vikings were raiders. Most lived peaceably at home, farming, hunting, fishing and trading. They were excellent sailors and had been trading around the coasts of the Baltic Sea and the North Sea for centuries before they took to raiding southern lands.

The earliest Viking traders had used certain convenient spots as meeting points for doing deals and exchanging goods. In time these places developed into permanent markets. A local chieftain or king would agree to protect a market from attack (mostly from other piratical Vikings) in return for a tax on its trade. This gave him an interest in encouraging the market's growth. In this way several Viking markets grew into sizable towns. This is your guide to a typical Viking town at some time in the 9th or 10th century.

AROUND THE TOWN

Feasting Viking life is hard and the climate cold. To be snug indoors with lots to eat and drink is the best of treats – join a family as they enjoy a feast and get-together on pages 34 and 35.

Town defences
The first thing that strikes you about the town is the earth rampart that surrounds it. The townspeople must be afraid of attacks from outside. Learn the reasons why on pages 20 and 21.

Farming
Beyond the ramparts are the many little farms that use every patch of fertile land. They are the basis of Viking life for they grow the food for everyone and you can see how they do it on pages 28 and 29.

Getting around
You'll want to see as much as possible on your visit, but travel isn't easy. Roads are few and many are rough. Going by boat is simpler since all towns are close to water. Find out more on pages 30 and 31.

Slave trading
At the slave market foreign-looking men and women are for sale. Some of them have been captured in war, others have been snatched from their homes by Viking raiders. For sights you won't see at home go to pages 26 and 27!

Shipbuilding
Watch Viking shipbuilders at work on pages 22 and 23. No one builds better boats. The Vikings' warships are fast, light, flexible and strong enough to withstand high seas, yet can be navigated in very shallow water.

Homes
The houses in the town are built of wood. Most are set with the gable end to the street and have a small fenced yard with a well. You'll have a good view of one on pages 14 and 15.

Burial
The Vikings bury their dead in the cemetery just outside the town. The wealthy have some of their best possessions buried with them, for use in the next world. Be respectful, but you could watch a funeral on pages 32 and 33.

Merchants
Merchants flock to the town's market. Many have been to distant lands in search of goods – fur, walrus ivory and amber from further north; textiles, wines, ornaments and damascened swords from the south. You'll find many things to buy on pages 18 and 19.

Crafts
The town is a manufacturing centre where craftworkers produce and sell the things that are difficult for most people to make themselves – weapons, cooking pots, leather goods and so on. Join the throng of buyers on pages 16 and 17.

Raiders
Some ships may be off to raid a foreign target. Their owners hope to return with lots of loot – gold and silver, and people to sell as slaves. Watch a raiding party depart on pages 24 and 25.

The harbour
The waterfront is always busy. There is a constant bustle as trading vessels are loaded and unloaded, fishermen bring in their catch and longships are fitted out for expeditions. Be one of the crowd on pages 12 and 13.

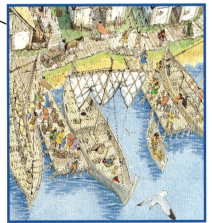

AT THE HARBOUR

This is most visitors' first view of the town, for long-distance travellers normally arrive by boat. Viking towns are always near the water, either the river or the sea, for towns flourish where people come to trade, and traders use the waterways because there are few roads. You can see what a busy place this is. The jetties are crowded. A ship with a cargo of Rhenish wine is being unloaded at one. At another a foreign merchant checks each item as the goods he has just bought in the town are taken aboard his vessel. A farmer from along the coast is bringing produce to market in his little home-built boat.

Viking boats can be beached in very shallow water, enabling the occupants to leap easily ashore.

Knorrs, which are shorter and broader than the longboats used for raiding, are well adapted for transporting all kinds of cargo.

Jetty

Additional mooring for smaller boats

Along the waterfront wooden jetties provide unloading space for as many craft as possible. You can see (left) how jetties are constructed over the water. Within the harbour the sea is quite calm. If a port lacks the shelter of a natural headland it is protected from rough seas by an artificial one – a curved embankment of stones and earth.

A Family at Home

The best houses, in the middle the of town, are quite large by Viking standards, each with a patch of land and perhaps an outside storehouse and a well. Yet many of them are just a single room with a beaten earth floor, a stone-lined hearth in the middle of the room and a hole in the roof to let the smoke out. The roofs are thatched; the walls are made of planks or of wattle (uprights infilled with interwoven hazel twigs). The wattle is coated with clay to keep out draughts. Furniture is sparse – some stools, a table and chests and barrels for storage; beds are made up on a raised earth bench along the wall. Even so, with large families there is no room to spare. Grandparents, parents and all the unmarried children share this living space for cooking, eating, sleeping and entertaining. It is their workplace too. Here they spin, weave, sew clothes, preserve food for winter, repair the tools used for outdoor work and make things for sale.

These parents are wearing fine clothes for a feast. The mother's decorated overdress is pinned with silver brooches. She would wear a plain overdress for everyday.

All clothes are made at home. Against the wall is the loom on which the cloth is woven. Men and women wear woollen tunics, over which women sometimes wear an unbelted, open-sided overdress. Men wear trousers, bound round the legs or loose. Long cloaks, fur-lined for the rich, keep out the cold in winter.

Viking household goods: 1 Whalebone board and glass ball for smoothing clothes after washing. 2 Soapstone bowl. 3 Trough to mix bread dough. 4 Striker to make sparks to light fires. 5 Implement for cooking fish. 6 Wooden bucket.

WHAT'S MADE IN TOWN

There is one street in the town which is always busy and noisy. This is where the workshops are. Blacksmiths and coopers can't help making a din with their hammering, and leather tanning is a smelly business, so most workshops are grouped in one area. The craftworkers set up stalls outside their houses, so this is where everyone comes to shop. Metalwork, leather goods and carving in bone and amber are specialities. People buy direct from the makers; for horse-harness they go to the saddler, for shoes, belts and purses to the soft-leather workers, for lamps and bowls to the soapstone carvers. All sorts of metal goods are sold, from iron tools, locks and cooking pots to really skilled work, such as magnificent brooches of silver or gold.

Cheaper brooches are mass-produced like this: 1 Clay is pressed onto a good brooch to make the front of the mould. 2 This half is lined with clay-soaked cloth. More clay is added to form the back of the mould. 3 The halves are separated, the cloth removed, the mould reassembled and molten metal poured into the gap left by the cloth. 4 The cast of the metal brooch after it has cooled.

Celtic-style brooch (top left) with its owner's name in runes (Viking letters). A silver brooch (above) to hold a cloak in place. Glass beads (left) are made by melting broken glass, forming it into sticks of different colours and then twisting several sticks round a rod to make the hole. The rod is removed and the new glass stick cut across into beads.

Soapstone is soft and easy to make into bowls (top). Other craftsmen carve jewellery from Baltic amber (below).

Soapstone mould (top) and the dragon-headed ornament cast in it. Carved antler and bone objects: antler comb made in several pieces joined with pins (above), name tag marked in runes and a bone pin (far left).

THE MERCHANTS' CAMP

Many Viking merchants risk their lives for profit, making long and dangerous voyages in search of goods to trade. Some sail to northernmost Norway and Finland to bring back bear skins and walrus ivory. Others travel eastwards to the Slavs' lands. From there they begin the long river journey through Russia to the trading town of Kiev – a long and risky trip, but worth it to meet Arab traders with silver to spend and eastern luxuries to sell.

If you are looking for luxury goods you'll find them in the open area near the rampart, where the visiting merchants camp. Each spreads his wares in front of his tent and the bargaining is brisk. All sorts of goods change hands here, bought by traders who will resell them elsewhere. Many merchants come from the south, some Franks, some Frisians, some returning Vikings. They sell Byzantine silks and glass, eastern spices, fine woollen cloth from Frisia, wine and pottery from the Rhineland and Frankish sword blades, which are prized as the best. They'll spend the profits on the northern goods that fetch high prices in the south – honey, beeswax, furs and slaves.

Foreign luxuries for wealthy Vikings: furs from the north; a glass vase and beaker from the Rhineland and a roll of eastern silk that must have passed through many traders' hands on its way to the west.

Statue of Buddha from northern India. Probably bought there by a trader travelling the overland 'Silk Road' between China and the west which crossed the Vikings' north-south river route at Kiev.

Bowl from Constantinople (left). Few Vikings go so far east, but an Arab trader may have brought it to Kiev.

A Persian brazier and cup and a Byzantine silver bowl full of expensive oriental spices (left). 10th-century silver Viking coins (right). Viking currency is new. Payment is usually made in any form of silver – bars, rings, brooches, foreign coins – and the agreed amount is weighed out on the spot.

Silver-mounted rock crystal pendants, perhaps bought at a Slav trading post in northern Russia.

A silver locket (above), possibly from Baghdad.

DEFENDING THE TOWN

The strong rampart that surrounds the town allows its people to sleep securely at night without fear of a surprise attack. There is always the chance that Vikings from another region might make a raid. Or the Saxons or Frisians might be planning an invasion – perhaps in retaliation for Viking raids on their own towns and villages. If war comes, the town will provide a safe refuge for country people who have to flee from their unprotected farms. The king of this region is very willing to protect the town because the tax on its trade puts money in his coffers. He has financed the building of its roads and walls and is planning to give it even better defences. He is also organizing the building of a long earthwork to the south, which will protect the frontier.

House walls: poles are interwoven with hazel twigs and the inner face is coated with clay.

Thatching: rows of reed or straw bundles are fixed to the roof battens.

Building a house: timber uprights are set firmly into the ground. Then the roof timbers are added and the roof is thatched. The walls are infilled with wattle and daub or wooden staves. A gap at the top of the gable gives ventilation. Windows are rare.

Country roads are just earth tracks but the road out of town and all the main streets are paved with wood. Viking road-making is very rough: planks or split logs are laid over a wooden framework. On smaller paths wattle fencing is laid on the ground. This helps to keep feet out of the mud.

THE SHIPYARD

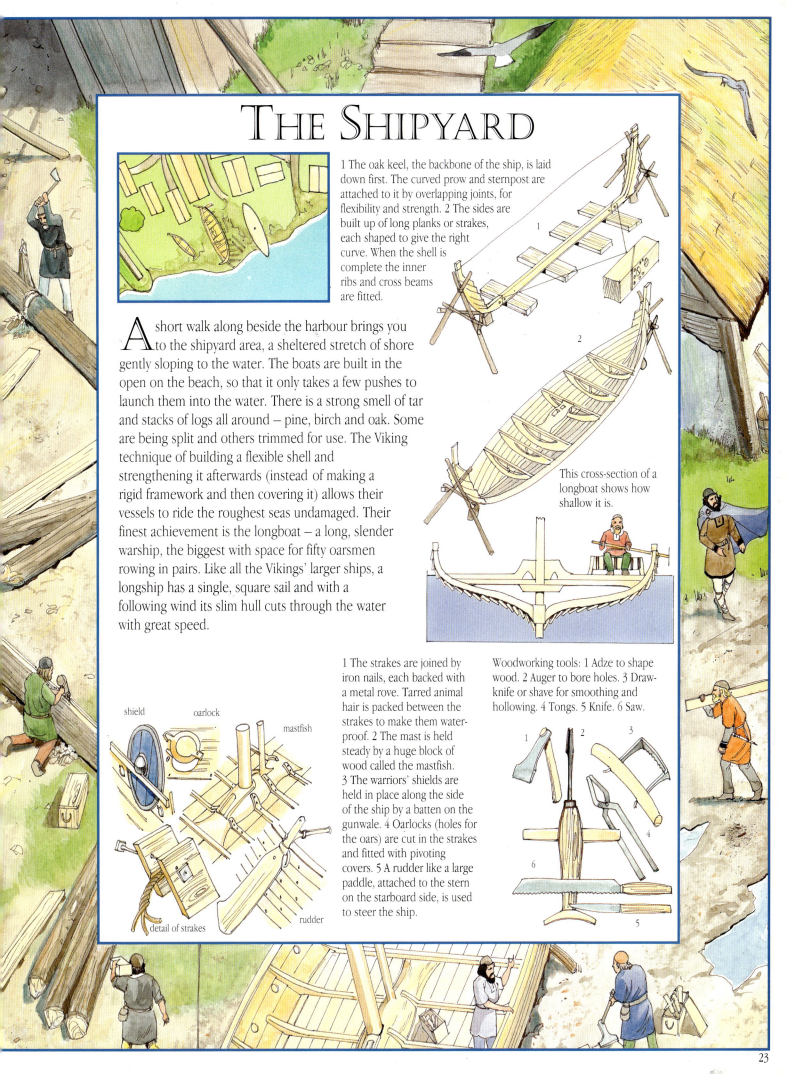

1 The oak keel, the backbone of the ship, is laid down first. The curved prow and sternpost are attached to it by overlapping joints, for flexibility and strength. 2 The sides are built up of long planks or strakes, each shaped to give the right curve. When the shell is complete the inner ribs and cross beams are fitted.

A short walk along beside the harbour brings you to the shipyard area, a sheltered stretch of shore gently sloping to the water. The boats are built in the open on the beach, so that it only takes a few pushes to launch them into the water. There is a strong smell of tar and stacks of logs all around – pine, birch and oak. Some are being split and others trimmed for use. The Viking technique of building a flexible shell and strengthening it afterwards (instead of making a rigid framework and then covering it) allows their vessels to ride the roughest seas undamaged. Their finest achievement is the longboat – a long, slender warship, the biggest with space for fifty oarsmen rowing in pairs. Like all the Vikings' larger ships, a longship has a single, square sail and with a following wind its slim hull cuts through the water with great speed.

This cross-section of a longboat shows how shallow it is.

1 The strakes are joined by iron nails, each backed with a metal rove. Tarred animal hair is packed between the strakes to make them water-proof. 2 The mast is held steady by a huge block of wood called the mastfish. 3 The warriors' shields are held in place along the side of the ship by a batten on the gunwale. 4 Oarlocks (holes for the oars) are cut in the strakes and fitted with pivoting covers. 5 A rudder like a large paddle, attached to the stern on the starboard side, is used to steer the ship.

Woodworking tools: 1 Adze to shape wood. 2 Auger to bore holes. 3 Draw-knife or shave for smoothing and hollowing. 4 Tongs. 5 Knife. 6 Saw.

shield

oarlock

mastfish

detail of strakes

rudder

A RAIDING PARTY

Among the cargo and fishing vessels that come and go in the harbour you may from time to time see a boatload of determined-looking armed men setting sail. This will be one of the raiding parties the Vikings have found so profitable. A wealthy Viking jarl with a longship gets together a group of men to make a swift sea-crossing to England or Scotland, Ireland or France. These Christian lands are prosperous; their unguarded monasteries are full of precious things. The Vikings make a lightning attack, seize all the goods and people they can, and are off to sea again before any resistance can be organized. Coastal areas are prime targets but inland towns are at their mercy too, for the shallow longships can go far upriver.

Reliquaries, caskets that hold the bones of a saint, are prized booty. This one (far left) was taken from an Irish or Scottish monastery. The animal-headed lead weight (left) came from Ireland.

Each man stows his gear in the chest on which he sits to row. Helmets and chainmail are only for wealthy jarls. Most raiders rely on a sword or an axe and a wooden shield.

The Vikings' shallow boats are very useful for raiding. The boats can be run onto the beach and the raiders leap ashore taking their victims by surprise. Those who resist are killed and any who are captured will be sold as slaves.

BUYING LIVESTOCK

The Vikings get the best prices for their slaves if they sell them further south – in Kiev for instance. The Arab dealers at the market there give large amounts of silver for slaves. These and furs are the main goods they buy in the northern markets.

Town and country are very close; it is a common sight to see cattle or goats being driven through the streets. They are on their way to the market where livestock is bought and sold. Men and women are on sale there too, as slaves. Vikings keep slaves to do the hard work. They have no rights; they may not own land, carry weapons or vote. Some of the people for sale are Vikings who were born as thralls (because their parents were – 'thral' is the Viking term for someone without the status of a freeman).

Raiders cannot fail to make a profit, for if they find nothing else worth taking there are always people. Anyone fit and fairly young is seized – and women are always in demand. Rich people are well worth taking for the ransom that can be demanded for returning them safely. In 841, for example, a French abbey paid 26 pounds (about 11.5 kilos) of silver to get some captives back.

But most are foreign. Some are Slavs captured on trading trips in the northern Baltic or in Russia (where Vikings traders turn to raiding to increase their stock of things to sell). Others are loot from Christian lands. Slaves are the town's most profitable export. There is a huge demand for them in the south. Many are bought by specialist slave traders and will change hands many times before reaching Baghdad in the east or the slave markets of the Mediterranean.

IN THE COUNTRY

As well as the food they grow, such as cabbages, wheat, barley (which does better than wheat in the cool climate), plums and apples, the Vikings collect wild fruits such as blackberries and nuts.

If you leave town by the inland road you soon pass farms on either side. Wherever the soil is good the ground has been cleared for fields and pasture and there are clusters of farm buildings. In places they form little villages. Farmhouses are often quite big long buildings, housing both the family and the men and thralls who help with the farm work. There is usually a barn for storage, where the cattle are sheltered in winter. Because country people need to be self-sufficient many farmers have their own smithy as well, where they make and mend tools. This is the way most Vikings live, growing what they eat and making everything they use; very few are town dwellers. Yet the town depends on the countryside for many things – for food from the farmers, furs and hides from the hunters and trappers, bog-iron from the marshes and timber from the forests.

A farming family must have enough land to live on. In some areas there is not enough to go round. Younger sons, who will not inherit the family farm, sometimes follow the example of the raiders – they cross the seas, take whatever land they can, whether inhabited or not, and settle there.

Spring is the time to plough and sow, as most Vikings live where the climate is too harsh for winter-sown crops. In the far north wheat will not grow at all.

Churning milk with a paddle to make butter is hard work. The women also preserve food for winter use, making cheeses, drying fish and salting meat.

1 Sickle for harvesting grain crops like wheat or barley. 2 Shears for clipping sheep. 3 Quern for the endless task of grinding flour for bread.

Sheep and goats are the main source of milk. Unlike cows, sheep can survive on the grass that grows on poor or rocky soil. And goats will eat anything!

TRAVELLING ABOUT

Long distance travel is risky. Merchants travel in small, well armed groups for fear of attack. Their goods make them a target for raiders, but local people making short journeys are fairly safe. Those with horses to spare ride, if not they walk. Goods go by packhorse or cart. Winter, when the rivers and marshes are frozen and the hill slopes are smooth with snow, is almost the best time to travel. People use skis or skates and can take all sorts of short cuts. Sledges carrying goods skim over the snow much faster and more smoothly than carts.

Though there are wooden bridges in some places, the usual way to cross a river is to wade through at a ford – a shallow spot. Sometimes rune stones are set up on a river's bank to guide strangers to a bridge across it.

Skates are made from bone. This one (far right) is made from a horse's leg bone. A light sledge for two (right). Two-horse sledges are used for heavier loads. In winter the horses' shoes are fitted with crampons to stop them slipping.

Some carts have a detachable body (below) which can be lifted off and transferred to a boat, so that the goods being shipped do not need to be unloaded and reloaded.

BEYOND THE GRAVE

Thor's hammer

The grassy slope to the north, outside the rampart, is the town's burial ground. Here the dead are laid to rest, surrounded by their prized possessions which are buried with them, ready for use in the next world, for Vikings believe in a life after death. Those who die in battle join Odin's band of warriors who live with him in Valhalla, his golden hall in Asgard, the land beyond the rainbow bridge. Odin, god of battle, is king of the many gods and goddesses who live there. He is a mysterious, rather frightening figure. Fiery-tempered Thor, the hammer-wielding thunderer, is more popular. People call to him when danger threatens. There is talk in the town of a new god who is greater than either Odin or Thor – the god the Christians worship. The Frankish missionaries who arrived some time ago have built a little wooden church and made a few converts. They would make more if they did not insist that people gave up their old gods on becoming Christian. Most Vikings are reluctant to do this; they want the best of both worlds. But they will have to change eventually, for when their rulers are converted they will want all their people to be Christian, too.

Objects like these are buried with their wealthy owners.
1. Part of a horse's bridle made of gilded metal. 2. Woman's dress ornament made of gilt-bronze. 3. One of a pair of gilt-bronze brooches inlaid with coloured enamels.

Some graves are marked by stones set out in the form of a ship, as if death were a voyage.

Pagan Viking funeral customs vary from place to place. Some people bury their dead; others burn them. Great chiefs may travel to the next world in a real boat, with horses, goods, weapons and even servants laid beside them. The boat is then either set alight or buried in a pit with earth piled over it.

In 922 an Arab described the funeral of a Viking chief he saw by the Volga in Russia. The chief and his possessions were put in a tent on the boat's deck and a slave girl was killed and put beside him. Then the boat was set alight.